Little Pebble™

Colorful Foods

Green Foods

by Martha E. H. Rustad

CAPSTONE PRESS
a capstone imprint

Little Pebble is published by Capstone Press,
1710 Roe Crest Drive, North Mankato, Minnesota 56003
www.mycapstone.com

Library of Congress Cataloging-in-Publication Data
Names: Rustad, Martha E. H. (Martha Elizabeth Hillman), 1975– author.
Title: Green foods / by Martha E. H. Rustad.
Description: North Mankato, Minnesota: Capstone Press, [2017] | Series:
Little pebble. Colorful foods | Audience: Ages 4–7. | Audience: K to grade 3. | Includes bibliographical references and index.
Identifiers: LCCN 2016009745| ISBN 9781515723721 (library binding) | ISBN 9781515723769 (pbk.) | ISBN 9781515723806 (ebook (pdf)
Subjects: LCSH: Food—Juvenile literature. | Green—Juvenile literature. |
Color of food—Juvenile literature.
Classification: LCC TX355 .R854 2017 | DDC 641.3—dc23
LC record available at http://lccn.loc.gov/2016009745

Editorial Credits
Megan Atwood, editor; Juliette Peters, designer;
Jo Miller, media researcher; Steve Walker, production specialist

Photo Credits
Images by Capstone Studio: Karon Dubke
Photo styling: Sarah Schuette and Marcy Morin

Printed and bound in China.

PO007712LEOF16

Table of Contents

Green Foods

What does the color green taste like? Let's think of green foods.

Green Fruits

Grapes grow on vines.

They taste sweet.

Limes taste sour.

Put slices in water.

Sip!

Here is a fuzzy kiwi.

Inside it is green.

Green Vegetables

Kale is curly.

We eat it raw.

Crunch!

Peapods hang from stems.

Pop!

Find peas inside.

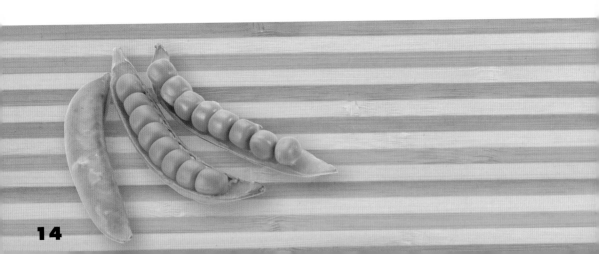

Broccoli grows up
from the ground.
We eat the flower.

Green Meals

We make salad for lunch.

The lettuce is green.

My aunt cuts an avocado.

We make tacos.

Yum!

What other foods are green?

Glossary

flower—a plant part that grows out of the stem

fuzzy—covered in short fibers or hair

slice—a piece cut from something bigger

stem—the main part of a plant

taco—a Mexican food that is a corn or flour shell with filling

vine—a long plant stem

Read More

Heos, Bridget. *So You Want to Grow a Salad?* Grow Your Food. Mankato, Minn.: Amicus, 2016.

Nunn, Daniel. *Green.* Colors All Around Us. Chicago: Heinemann-Raintree, 2012.

O'Connell, Emma. *We Love Green!* Our Favorite Colors. New York: Gareth Stevens Publishing, 2016.

Internet Sites

FactHound offers a safe, fun way to find Internet sites related to this book. All of the sites on FactHound have been researched by our staff.

Here's all you do:
Visit *www.facthound.com*
Type in this code: 9781515723721

Check out projects, games and lots more at
www.capstonekids.com

Index